Unbelievable Pictures and Facts About Bahamas

By: Olivia Greenwood

Introduction

The Bahamas is a beautiful holiday destination. It is also a fascinating place to live. Today we will be learning all about the beautiful Bahamas and everything that it has to offer.

What point is the highest in the Bahamas?

The tallest point in the Bahamas has got to an area called Mount Alvernia.

What is the most commonly spoken language in the Bahamas?

Although you may find people speaking all sorts of the languages, the official language in the country is English.

Does the Bahamas have a particular national bird?

Have you ever heard of the flamingo bird? This bird is pink in color and it has long thin legs. The flamingo is considered to be the national bird of the country.

Will you find any reefs?

The answer is a big yes. You certainly will find some reefs in the Bahamas. In fact, the country is home to the third biggest barrier reef.

Which sport is the most popular in the country?

Can you guess which sport they love the most in the Bahamas? The answer is basketball.

What products do they export from the Bahamas?

The Bahamas is known for exporting many different products. The main exports are cargo ships and petroleum.

Which religions do they practice in the Bahamas?

In the Bahamas, they practice all sorts of different religions. The most practiced religion is Christianity.

Is the Bahamas a very popular place to visit?

The Bahamas is a very popular place to visit. People really enjoy coming to the Bahamas and exploring the different islands.

What kinds of food do people eat in the country?

They eat all sorts of food in the Bahamas. One of the popular foods to eat is seafood. The entire country has lots of water and sea life.

Does the Bahamas have a national flower?

The Bahamas does have a national flower. The national flower is called the Yellow Elder and it is native to the area.

What financial currency do they use in the Bahamas?

If you want to travel to the Bahamas you may need to know what financial currency they use. The name of the financial currency used in the country is the Bahamian Dollar.

What is the population size in the Bahamas?

The Bahamas is home to only 393,400 people. Although this amount is growing each and every year, it remains on 177th in terms of population ranking.

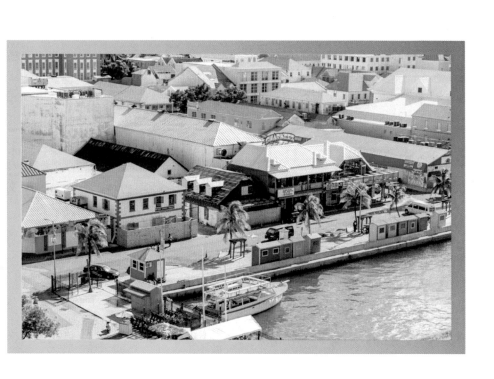

What is the name of the capital of the Bahamas?

The capital city is known as Nassau. It is home to over 250,000 people.

How many islands make up the Bahamas?

There are over 700 distinct islands which make up the Bahamas.

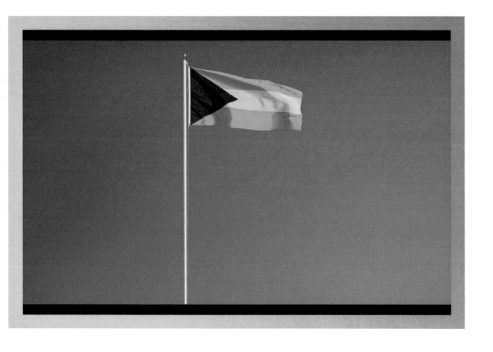

Will you find any animals in the Bahamas?

If you like animals, then you will be pleased to know that the Bahamas is filled with all sorts of wildlife and animal species. You will certainly find some animals that you won't find anywhere else in the world like the Bahamian parrot.

What type of weather will you experience in the Bahamas?

The type of weather which you will experience in the Bahamas is warm. The sun shines for most of the year. During the winter months, it does have a tendency to become very cold and rainy.

Is the Bahamas rich or poor?

The Bahamas is considered to be a very rich country. It is actually one of the richest countries in the West Indies.

Is it safe to travel in the Bahamas?

The answer is a big yes. It is generally very safe to travel in the Bahamas. It is just important to remember that some of the islands are safer than others.

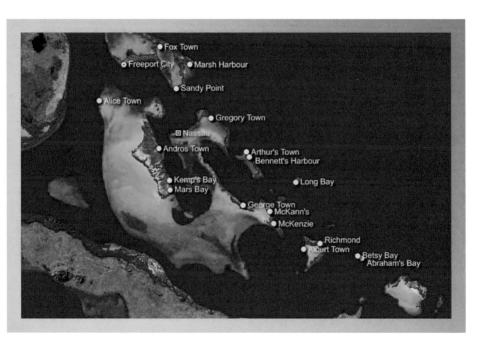

What type of landscape does the Bahamas have?

The Bahamas is known for its beautiful landscape. It is surrounded by hundreds of magnificent islands.

Where in the world is the Bahamas situated?

The Bahamas is part of the continent in North America. It is situated very close to the Atlantic sea.

Made in the USA
Middletown, DE
11 December 2022

18033758R00024